OPERATION RESCUE

SATELLITE MAINTENANCE AND REPAIR

BY D.J. HERDA

FRANKLIN WATTS
NEW YORK/LONDON/TORONTO/SYDNEY/1990
A FIRST BOOK

Cover photograph, showing two astronauts securing the *Palapa P-2* communications satellite to the space shuttle *Discovery*'s cargo bay in November 1984, comes courtesy of NASA.

All photographs courtesy of NASA, except: Sovfoto/Tass: p. 50.

Library of Congress Cataloging-in-Publication Data

Herda, D. J., 1948–

Operation rescue : satellite maintenance and repair / by D. J. Herda.
p.   cm. — (A First book)
Includes bibliographical references.
Summary: Describes those rendezvous in space during which repairs
were made to satellites and spacecraft.
ISBN 0-531-10873-2
1. Artificial satellites—Maintenance and repair—Juvenile
literature.   2. Space rescue operations—Juvenile literature.
[1. Artificial satellites—Maintenance and repair.   2. Space rescue
operations.]   I. Title.   II. Series.
TL915.H37   1990
629.46′028′8—dc20   90-12369   CIP   AC

CONTENTS

On October 4, 1957, the Soviet Union lifted the first artificial satellite into orbit around the earth. *Sputnik 1* marked the birth of the Space Age.

In November, the Soviets lifted *Sputnik 2* into orbit. Aboard was the first living passenger—a dog named Laika. The craft was equipped with instruments to monitor the animal's condition in the weightlessness of space.

In the United States, amidst fears that the Soviets were gaining too much ground in the quest to conquer space, the U.S. Defense Department decided to launch America's first satellite. Within two months, on January 31, 1958, the United States Army launched *Explorer 1* into space aboard a *Jupiter C* rocket. The satellite weighed just 31 pounds (14 kg) and measured 6.7 feet (2.03 m). It was the first time the American flag had left the earth's atmosphere.

The race for space was on.

One of the newest satellites
is the *Galileo* spacecraft,
which began its six-year
journey to the planet
Jupiter in October 1989.
It is shown here after
it was detached from the
space shuttle *Atlantis*.

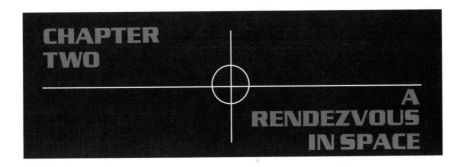

From early on in the United States space program, NASA (National Aeronautics and Space Administration) had been sending satellites into orbit around the earth in increasing numbers. These included communication satellites that carry television, radio, and telephone signals; scientific and research satellites that help us to predict the weather, conduct experiments in the weightlessness of space, and learn about the world we live in; and military satellites that provide valuable information for the country's defenses.

As early as 1965, NASA officials realized that a future space mission would require astronauts to retrieve damaged or malfunctioning satellites for repair back on earth. In order to bring back and repair these satellites, NASA needed to develop a program to allow two or more vehicles to rendezvous—or come together—in space. The ability to rendezvous in space would not only make satellite repair and

An astronaut approaches the spinning *Westar VI* satellite, with the Bahamas in the far background.

A communications satellite
drifts in space, moments
after it was released
from the cargo bay
of the space
shuttle *Discovery*

reuse possible, but it would also prevent American astronauts from being stranded in space by a serious accident.

On August 21, 1965, astronauts USAF Lt. Col. Gordon Cooper and Navy Lt. Cmdr. Charles "Pete" Conrad, Jr., blasted into orbit. Their mission was to test the navigational system for rendezvousing their *Gemini 5* spacecraft with several target vehicles. These consisted of satellites launched earlier, with which *Gemini* hoped to link up.

Although problems with *Gemini*'s power system took up most of the crew's time and prevented an actual rendezvous, the crew was able to stage an imaginary link-up, that is, it managed to catch a make-believe point in orbit after executing several complicated maneuvers.

On December 4, 1965, *Gemini 7*, carrying astronauts USAF Lt. Col. Frank Borman and Navy Cmdr. James A. Lovell, Jr., was lifted into orbit. It was followed shortly by *Gemini 6* with Navy Capt. Walter

Astronauts Conrad and Cooper check out the *Gemini 5* spacecraft for their 8-day orbital mission.

M. Schirra, Jr., and USAF Maj. Thomas P. Stafford on board. As both spacecraft circled the globe, astronaut Schirra in *Gemini 6* told the ground crew that his radar had locked onto *Gemini 7* during its third orbit. An hour later, Schirra exclaimed, "My gosh, there's a real bright star out there." The star was actually *Gemini 7*, reflecting sunlight in the blackness of space.

Later, after chasing its target a few times around the earth, *Gemini 6* crept to within 1 foot (0.3 m) of *Gemini 7*. The two orbiting spacecraft circled the world together several times before returning to earth.

In March 1966, NASA launched *Gemini 8* hot on the heels of an unmanned *Agena* target vehicle. "Flight, we are docked!" It was civilian astronaut Neil A. Armstrong radioing back to ground control from *Gemini 8*, announcing that the rendezvous was completed. "It's . . . really a smoothie—no noticeable oscillations [vibrations] at all," he said.

But Armstrong had spoken too soon. Within thirty minutes, the two spacecraft began spinning out of control. The trouble began when the gauges on the control panel showed that *Gemini* was in a 30-degree roll. Fellow astronaut USAF Maj. David R. Scott knew the gauges should show level flight. He tried calling ground control, but the spacecraft was

Gemini 8 liftoff

on the far side of the globe, high above China, and out of communication range. Armstrong tried to stop the roll by using the maneuvering thruster rockets, but that only made the spin worse.

Believing the problem to be with the Agena target vehicle, Scott hit the undocking button and Armstrong gave the thruster a long burst to pull *Gemini 8* free of its target. Once separated, *Gemini 8* began spinning even faster. The two astronauts suddenly realized that the problem wasn't in the target vehicle at all, but in their own spacecraft!

Armstrong finally made contact with a tracking ship off the coast of China. "We're toppling end over end, but we're disengaged from Agena. . . . We can't turn anything off."

The ship relayed the message to Houston Flight Control. "He seems to be in a pretty violent tumble," the ship's radio operator reported.

Soon, *Gemini* was revolving once a second, nearly twice as fast as a 33^1/$_3$ RPM record on a turntable. The astronauts felt dizzy at first, then their vision began to blur. They were coming close to blacking out. If they lost consciousness, the spacecraft would continue to spin faster and faster. The result could be deadly.

There was nothing left to do . . . almost nothing.

"All we've got left is the reentry control system,"

Armstrong radioed. He turned off the thruster switches and activated the reentry control system, normally used only when the spacecraft prepares for reentry and splashdown. It was a desperate, last-ditch effort, and both men prayed it would work.

Slowly, the hand controllers began to respond—the spinning spacecraft began to slow. Gradually, Gemini 8 was coming under control.

When the spacecraft passed within communication range of the Hawaii tracking station, ground control ordered Armstrong and Scott to make an emergency landing in the Pacific Ocean. A short while later, two dazed but thankful astronauts splashed down safely 500 miles (805 km) west of Okinawa, Japan. They had gambled with death and won.

NASA tests later showed that one of Gemini 8's maneuver thrusters had stuck open—"failed on," in space talk. That simple malfunction nearly cost two men their lives.

Even though Gemini 8's mission had to be shortened, it was considered a success. The spacecraft had completed an in-space rendezvous and docking with its Agena target vehicle launched just two hours earlier. What had nearly become the world's first space tragedy ended instead as the first successful docking of two orbiting vehicles in space.

CHAPTER THREE

STEPPING INTO SPACE

On June 3, 1966, astronauts USAF Lt. Col. Thomas P. Stafford and Navy Lt. Cmdr. Eugene A. Cernan lifted off the launchpad in *Gemini 9A*, immediately behind an unmanned Agena target vehicle launched two days earlier.

During *Gemini's* third orbit, the spacecraft rendezvoused with the 12-foot (3.7-m) target, but the scheduled docking failed to take place. Cernan called the target vehicle an "angry alligator" because its protective covering was still attached; the halves opened like two giant jaws, preventing *Gemini* from a link-up.

Still, the astronauts practiced their rendezvous skills, and on June 5, Cernan put on his Astronaut Maneuvering Unit (AMU) and became the first American to step into space. Unfortunately, Cernan couldn't see because his breath caused his faceplate to fog up. His suit's air conditioner did not function properly. After less than an hour, the astronaut gave

An astronaut dangles in space, secured to his *Gemini 4* spacecraft by a gold cord. He is equipped with an emergency oxygen chest pad, a camera, and a hand-held device that gives him control over his movements in the zero gravity of space.

up and returned to the safety of the cockpit. His second spacewalk was more successful, lasting two hours and five minutes.

On July 18, 1966, *Gemini 10*, crewed by Navy Cmdr. John W. Young and USAF Maj. Michael Collins, blasted into space. It chased two Agena target vehicles—their own and the one still orbiting from the *Gemini 8* mission. *Gemini 10* rendezvoused with its Agena target just 5 hours, 21 minutes after launch. Once docked, the astronauts fired their powerful rockets, lifting both vehicles into a record-high 458-mile (761-k) orbit.

After 39 hours, *Gemini* undocked from its target. Two days later, Young and Collins guided their spacecraft to a rendezvous with the *Gemini 8* target vehicle. Collins opened the hatch and stepped out into space. He propelled himself with a gas-firing tool called a Zot gun until he reached the target, where he collected two scientific packages that scientists wanted to study back on earth.

After an EVA (extravehicular activity)—activity outside the spacecraft—that lasted 39 minutes, Collins returned to Gemini. It was the first successful EVA in the history of America's space program.

On September 12, 1966, *Gemini 11*, with crewmembers Charles "Pete" Conrad, Jr., and Navy Lt. Cmdr. Richard F. Gordon, Jr., lifted into space and

An astronaut rehearses a scheduled space activity.

caught their target vehicle during their very first orbit. The successful rendezvous was completed within one and one half hours.

During the second day of flight, Gordon began an EVA over Houston where he hitched a 100-foot (30.5-m) nylon line from *Gemini 11* to the Agena target vehicle to observe the reaction of the two spacecraft once they undocked. But the strain of working in space proved too much. Conrad's heart rate soared to 102 beats a minute, and his faceplate, like Cernan's of *Gemini 9*, fogged up so that he couldn't see. The EVA was ended just 44 minutes into the mission, less than half the planned time.

Despite such problems, NASA considered the Gemini program a success. It proved that not only could two spacecraft rendezvous in space, but that astronauts also could work outside their spacecraft.

Next, NASA looked forward to an even more ambitious goal—the moon. The program designed to get them there was named Apollo.

CHAPTER FOUR

TO THE MOON

On December 21, 1968, astronauts USAF Col. Frank Borman, James A. Lovell, Jr., and USAF Lt. Col. William A. Anders blasted off atop a powerful Saturn 5 rocket. More than a quarter of a million people were gathered to witness the launch as the rocket slowly climbed skyward on a column of fire as wide as a Naval battleship.

During *Apollo 8*'s second orbit over Hawaii, Mission Control communicator Michael Collins gave the order: "You are go." Within moments, *Apollo* crew commander Borman threw the switch igniting the giant rocket engine. The spacecraft's speed was boosted to 24,200 miles (38,938 k) an hour, the speed required to escape the pull of the earth's gravity. It was the fastest a human had ever traveled— more than 400 times faster than a car going 55 miles (88.5 k) an hour.

The *New York Times* described the mission as "the most fantastic voyage of all times." After a 57-

Apollo 11 liftoff

hour return flight, *Apollo 8* splashed down safely in the Pacific Ocean.

After similar successes with *Apollo 9* and *10*, NASA gave the go-ahead for *Apollo 11*, named *Columbia*, to blast off for a first-ever trip to the moon. Onboard, astronauts Neil A. Armstrong, USAF Col. Edwin Eugene "Buzz" Aldrin, Jr., and USAF Lt. Col. Michael Collins calmly checked their lists and prepared for a moon-landing.

On Sunday morning, July 20, 1969, with *Columbia* orbiting the moon, Armstrong and Aldrin climbed aboard their Lunar Excursion Module (LEM). The LEM was designed to undock from the command ship and take the astronauts from their orbiting spacecraft to the surface of the moon and back again. The LEM, nicknamed Eagle, fell into orbit right behind *Apollo*. "The Eagle has wings," Armstrong radioed to earth.

Finally, Houston gave Eagle the "go" for a descent to the moon. But five minutes into its descent, a yellow warning light in the cockpit came on.

"Program alarm!" Armstrong radioed back to earth. Within moments, Houston came back with another "go." The alarm was only a sign that Eagle's onboard computers were processing too much information at one time. A second alarm was similarly analyzed—followed by four more. Concerned by these warnings, the crew had little time to look out the cockpit windows. When they finally did, Armstrong saw that they were just minutes from a lunar landing. And Eagle was heading directly for a large boulder field surrounded by a huge crater! The boulders were large enough to rip open the belly of Eagle. Later, Houston reported that Armstrong's pulse had jumped to 156 beats a minute, more than twice its normal rate.

Suddenly Armstrong realized he would have to override the computer and manually control the moonship to avoid the boulder field. As Eagle drew to within 100 feet (30.5 m) of the moon, Armstrong spotted a small clearing about the size of an average house lot and headed for it. A red warning light went on. Only 5 percent of Eagle's descent fuel remained. If the LEM didn't land within 94 seconds, the astronauts would have to abort the landing and return to Apollo—or risk a crash landing on the moon.

Armstrong checked the gauges. Only 60 seconds of fuel left. The lunar dust kicked up by Eagle's engines clouded his view as he looked out the window, preventing him from judging his altitude and forward motion. The fuel gauge dropped to 30 seconds. Still Armstrong couldn't see. The gauge continued to drop as the pilot blindly maneuvered the vehicle to where he hoped Eagle could land safely.

Armstrong was so occupied with maneuvering the LEM that he didn't hear Aldrin call out "contact light" as the vehicle's footpad probes brushed the surface of the moon. They were down . . . with less than 20 seconds of fuel to spare!

Armstrong took a deep breath and radioed back to ground control, "Houston, Tranquility Base here. The Eagle has landed." As the moon-dust cleared, the blazing, bright moonscape burst upon them. Unbelievably, they had succeeded. They were the first humans in history to land on the moon.

Six and a half hours later, Armstrong opened Eagle's hatch and stepped out. At 10:56 P.M. Eastern Daylight Time, the astronaut descended the ladder, planted his left boot on the surface of the moon, and said simply, "That's one small step for a man, one giant leap for mankind."

As spectacular as the flight of *Apollo 11* had been, future Apollo missions were equally successful. Succeeding missions equipped each LEM with a Lunar Roving Vehicle (LRV), a moon-going dunebuggy used to transport the astronauts across the lunar surface, while the astronauts gained invaluable experience rendezvousing their LEMS and command ships.

NASA's final Apollo project, *Apollo 17*, was the last manned lunar-landing-and-exploration mission.

Astronaut Aldrin walks on the surface of the moon during the *Apollo 11* EVA.

Aldrin sets up two scientific experimental packages on the moon. The United States flag and the lunar module "Eagle" can be seen in the far background.

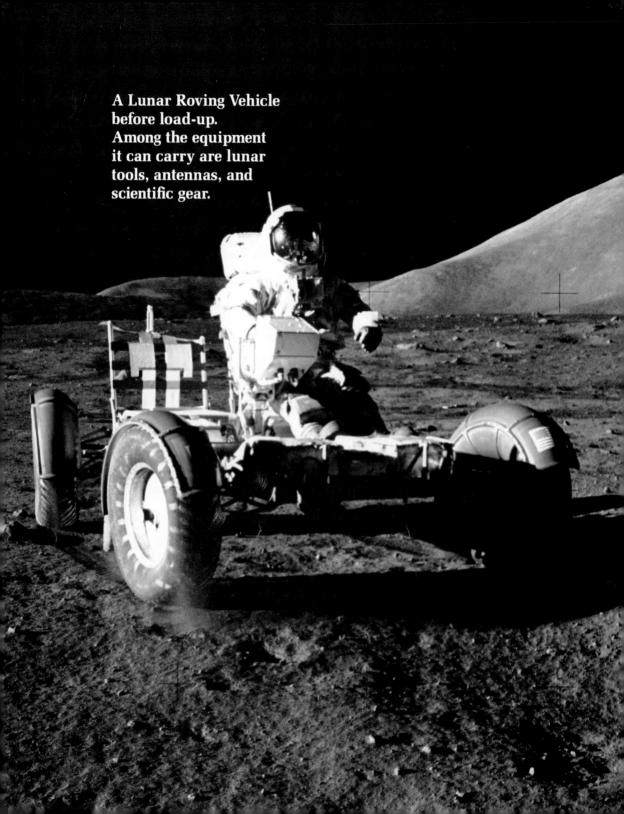

A Lunar Roving Vehicle
before load-up.
Among the equipment
it can carry are lunar
tools, antennas, and
scientific gear.

The ambitious Apollo program taught NASA engineers many things about EVA maneuvers, rendezvousing, and docking. Astronauts were able to practice the rescue and repair procedures so important to the success of future space exploration as well as the building of a permanent space station scheduled for the 1990s.

In the meantime, NASA set its sights on several more realistic goals. Next stop: the space shuttle.

CHAPTER FIVE

SHUTTLING AROUND

On April 12, 1981, *Columbia,* the first of the giant space shuttles was launched. A space shuttle is a fleet of four vehicles designed to fly numerous space missions. It carried with it a number of futuristic space appliances, like a Manned Maneuvering Unit (MMU). Looking like a small, legless chair, the MMU is strapped to an astronaut's back and operated by the flick of a wrist or finger on an armrest control panel. The pack allows an astronaut to move freely outside the spacecraft without being tied to the ship. For the first time ever, an astronaut would become a freely orbiting "satellite" moving more than 17,000 miles (27,353 km) an hour.

Although each MMU weighs 338 pounds (153 kg) on earth, it is weightless in space. Twenty-four jet thrusters on the unit move the astronaut through space, while heaters prevent the nitrogen gas that powers the thrusters from freezing in the −150° F (−101° C) temperatures of space.

Columbia liftoff

**Astronaut Robert L. Stewart glides in
space wearing his Manned Maneuvering
Unit (MMU) strapped on his back.**

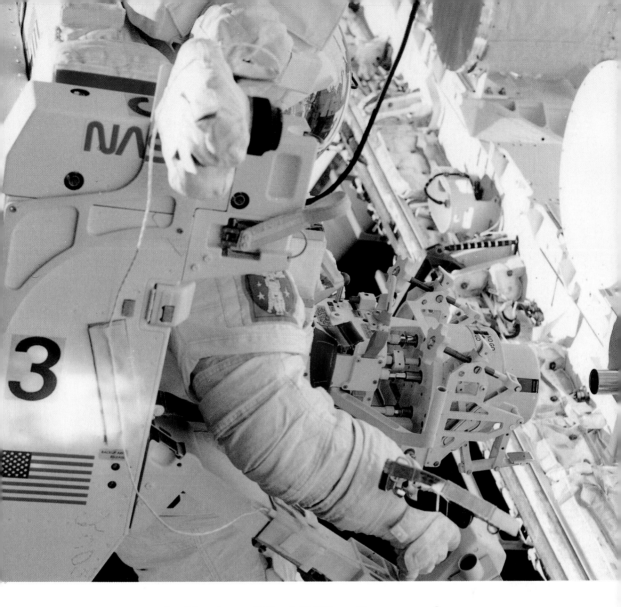

A side view of the MMU unit, as worn by
astronaut McCandless. He is shown
aligning an attachment device into
another special device on a satellite
in the *Challenger*'s cargo bay.

MMUs are expected to be used throughout the 1990s. Their many tasks include flying astronauts in and out of the beams of the space station due to be erected. Should an astronaut find himself stranded or in serious trouble, an MMU would bring another astronaut to the rescue.

After several years of testing, the MMU underwent its final challenge. On February 7, 1984, Bruce McCandless became the world's first untied space walker when he jetted out nearly 300 feet (91.5 m) from the space shuttle, *Challenger.* His life was completely dependent upon the equipment strapped to his back. It worked flawlessly.

Besides MMUs, shuttle spacecraft are equipped with giant robotic arms for various rescue and repair missions. A robotic arm can be 50 feet (15.2 m) long and weigh 900 pounds (408 kg). It can reach out and grab a satellite from space, place another into orbit, act as a foothold for astronauts reaching into space, and perform other tasks from its base in the shuttle's cargo bay.

The arm, known as a Remote Manipulator System (RMS), is built like a human arm, including a shoulder, elbow, wrist, and "hand" (NASA calls it an "end effector"). It is equipped with snare wires that can grab and hold a satellite or other object. The RMS's movements are controlled by electric motors

Bruce McCandless became the first person to walk in space untethered.

The "end effector" of the RMS aboard the shuttle *Discovery* is a hand-like device used to assist in the capture of stranded satellites.

McCandless "rides" the RMS arm during an EVA.

McCandless performs an experiment on a satellite, with his feet anchored to the RMS.

run by mission specialists operating a control panel in the aft, or rear, section of the shuttle's flight deck. Television cameras mounted on the RMS's wrist and elbow provide the operators with the view necessary for maneuvering the arm toward its target. When not in use, the RMS is latched inside the cargo bay.

In numerous shuttle flights, the RMS has proven very valuable. It has boosted astronauts to nearby satellites for retrieval, as when mission specialists Joseph P. Allen and Dale A. Gardner brought the ailing *Westar VI* satellite back to their shuttle's cargo bay for repairs. But not all such missions go so smoothly.

In April 1984, *Challenger* astronaut George D. Nelson jetted over to the wildly spinning Solar Maximum Mission satellite (Solar Max), a sophisticated scientific instrument designed to gather information about the energy output of the sun during its 11-year cycle of solar activity. The Solar Max had stopped working soon after it was launched and had been drifting uselessly in space since 1981. The tens of millions of dollars spent to develop and deploy the satellite were feared lost.

After three unsuccessful attempts to snag Solar Max, the satellite began spinning even faster. Nelson returned to *Challenger*, where mission commander

The gold-colored
Solar Max satellite
is temporarily docked
for repair aboard
the *Challenger*.

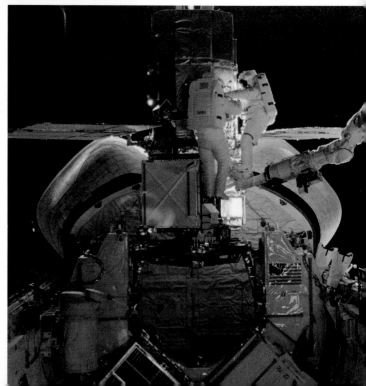

The ailing satellite
is repaired in the
shuttle's cargo bay.
Later, the RMS lifted
and returned the Solar
Max into space.

Aboard the *Columbia*, these astronauts
pose with a smile after successfully
deploying two commercial
communications satellites.

Robert L. Crippen tried to grab Solar Max with the RMS. That, too, failed.

Finally, on the fifth day, the astronauts were able to secure the satellite and pull it into the cargo bay, where Nelson and astronaut James D. van Hoften replaced its ailing control box. The next day, the RMS swung Solar Max back into orbit.

The world's first orbiting service call by the "Ace Satellite Repair Company," as the crew jokingly called themselves, had succeeded.

CHAPTER SIX

RESCUES IN SPACE

Not all satellite repairs take place in space. In November 1984, two communications satellites, Western Union's *Westar VI* and Indonesia's *Palapa B-2*, were plucked from space and given a ride back to earth aboard the space shuttle *Discovery*. Both satellites, launched from the space shuttle *Challenger* the preceding February, were stuck in uselessly low orbits with failed rocket motors.

Astronauts Joseph P. Allen and Dale A. Gardner retrieved *Palapa B-2* first, then went after *Westar VI*. But a protruding arm on *Westar* kept the astronauts from securing it to *Challenger*'s cargo bay.

Undaunted, Allen stood up into space with his feet strapped to the end of *Challenger*'s RMS and held the satellite between his hands while Gardner clamped it down to the bay. The procedure took one complete orbit, and Allen became the first person in history to hold a satellite suspended above his head for an entire trip around the world!

DO NOT TOUCH
SURFACE ATE

Astronaut Dale Gardner practices his
chores for a November 1984 EVA mission
aboard the *Challenger*, where he was
expected to retrieve two stranded
satellites. (Right) Gardner uses the
"stinger" device he has practiced with
to stabilize one of the satellites.

This photograph of the *Challenger*
over a cloudy portion of earth shows
its cargo bay, which was vacated by
two communications satellites.

The two satellites were eventually repaired and returned to orbit. The $10.5 million price tag for the rescue operation might have seemed costly, but it was only a fraction of the $70 million combined value of the satellites.

While American astronauts have logged numerous space rescue missions during the last decade, they're not alone. Several Soviet space travelers, called cosmonauts, have done the same.

Salyut 7, the giant Soviet space station launched in April 1982, provided the USSR with several space firsts. The crew of the spacecraft *Soyuz T-10B* set a world's space-endurance record by docking their *Soyuz* craft to *Salyut* and spending the next 237 days aboard the space station. One Soviet crew member, Svetlana Savitskaya, was the first woman to walk in space.

But *Salyut 7* had been overrun with problems. A year after deployment, *Salyut's* large, wing-like solar panels were barely generating enough energy to keep the station's life systems working. Cosmonauts Vladimir Lyakhov and Aleksandr Aleksandrov attached extra solar panels to the wings to correct the problem.

The same two cosmonauts were called upon later that year when a leak in *Salyut's* propulsion system sent Lyakhov and Aleksandrov scurrying for their

Cosmonaut engineer
Valentin Lebedev works
in open space outside
of the *Salyut 7* spacecraft.

lives to the safety of their *Soyuz* spacecraft. The two men needed five EVAs to repair the leak.

Soon after *Salyut 7*'s crew returned to earth, the space station began to deteriorate mysteriously. The Soviets asked mission commander Vladimir Djanibekov, a four-spacecraft veteran and cosmonaut of 15 years, and Viktor P. Savinykh, a *Salyut* expert and computer genius, to investigate.

When the cosmonauts crawled out of their spacecraft and into the orbiting station, they quickly realized that *Salyut*'s power system had failed and that its water system had frozen solid. Without action, *Salyut*'s orbit would continue to decay. Eventually the station would descend to an altitude where the atmosphere and earth's gravity would cause it to burst into a fiery ball.

While most experts believed *Salyut 7*'s life was over, the cosmonauts felt otherwise. They quickly rigged a makeshift ventilation system and repaired the station's batteries, six of which still showed signs of life. They worked mostly in 40-minute shifts during *Salyut*'s daytime passes of the sun, when the rays warmed the inside of the space station to −140 degrees F, before retreating to their *Soyuz* spacecraft to warm up.

For more than a week, the men continued working under the most difficult conditions ever experienced in space. Finally, the cosmonauts flipped on *Salyut's* lights, heaters, and equipment. Mission controllers outside Moscow cheered as the first data in six months began pouring into the center from a reborn *Salyut*. Djanibekov and Savinykh had brought a ghost ship back to life. *Salyut 7* had been saved.

More recently, U.S. space shuttle *Columbia* went on a rescue-and-retrieval mission of a disabled, 11-ton, bus-sized science satellite. The satellite, known as the *Long Duration Exposure Facility* (LDEF), was launched in 1984 to see how well various metals, plastics, glass, optical systems, and other materials survived during long periods in space. LDEF was scheduled to be retrieved after a year in orbit, but launch delays and the space shuttle *Challenger* disaster in January 1986, left it stranded.

Columbia was called on to retrieve LDEF on January 13, 1990, because the satellite had fallen into a steadily decaying orbit. If not recovered, it would plunge into destruction in the earth's atmosphere within two months. As Capt. Daniel C. Brandenstein, *Columbia's* mission commander, steered the ship manually toward the ailing satellite, mission specialist Dr. Bonnie J. Dunbar extended the robotic arm and snared the ailing satellite's grappling hook.

The *Challenger*'s RMS arm suspends the giant LDEF facility high above the Gulf of Mexico prior to its deployment in 1984.

With LDEF safely secured inside *Columbia's* cargo bay, Dr. Charles G. Simon, one of the researchers who would inspect LDEF after its return to earth, said, "This will give us more information about the environmental effects of space than all past space flights combined." Scientists expect this information to influence the design and construction of future spacecrafts.

CHAPTER SEVEN

THE FUTURE IS BRIGHT

Some day, space travel may be a precise science. As of today, it's not. Still, NASA officials continue to research, test, and evaluate new theories, new equipment, and new techniques. On the NASA drawing boards are several Orbit On Demand (OOD) vehicles capable of reaching distressed orbiting satellites in a matter of minutes rather than hours, weeks, or even months. Also in the works is a new tool developed by the Ford Motor Company, known as a Knowledge Engineering Environment (KEE). The KEE is designed to provide not only analyses of existing problems, but also solutions to anticipated problems.

So far, America and the world have been fortunate. Few fatalities have been recorded in the quest to conquer space. Several astronauts have lost their lives on the launching pad; seven others died tragically when the *Challenger* space shuttle exploded just 73 seconds after liftoff. Yet no one has been stranded in the deep, cold emptiness of space. For

[55]

An astronaut leans out into space a short distance from the *Westar VI* satellite.

that, NASA and the engineers of the world can be thanked.

Meanwhile, the work goes on. Scientists are working toward the day when a permanent orbiting space station, a permanent colony on the moon, and a manned trip to Mars will become a reality. Through it all, satellite rescue and repair missions and the brave crew members who execute them will continue to play a vital role.

GLOSSARY

Command module. A spacecraft compartment containing the crew and main controls.

Command ship. The spacecraft in which the command module exists.

Earth orbit. The path that a body, like a satellite, travels when acted upon by the earth's gravity.

Ground control. An earth-based center from which spacecraft are controlled and/or monitored.

Ground station. An earth-based transmitting and receiving station.

Liftoff. The beginning of a rocket's flight from its launchpad.

Lunar. Of or having to do with the moon.

NASA. National Aeronautics and Space Administration.

Planet. A satellite or star; the only known planets are those of the earth's sun, although others have been detected on nonobservational grounds around some of the stars nearer to earth.

Rocket. A space vehicle powered by rearward reacting combustion gases used to boost a spacecraft into orbit or beyond.

Salyut. A Soviet-built and manned orbiting space station.

Satellite. An object moving around a celestial body; the object may be either man-made or natural, like earth's moon.

Solar cell. A light-sensitive device that converts light rays into electrical energy.

Solar panel. A group of solar cells arranged in a series.

Soyuz. A Soviet-built manned spacecraft.

Spacecraft. A vehicle capable of traveling through space, often, although not always, manned.

Space station. A manned orbiting spacecraft capable of supporting habitation for long periods of time.

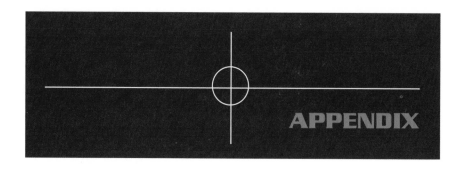

APPENDIX

Space Organizations

The groups below offer a variety of services and information for serious students of space and space travel. Call or write for more information.

American Astronautical Society
6212B Old Keene Mill Court
Springfield, VA 22152
(703) 866-0020

American Institute of Aeronautics
and Astronautics
Director of Student Programs
370 L'Enfant Promenade, SW
Washington, DC 20024
(202) 646-7432

National Space Club
655 15th St., NW
Washington, DC 20005
(202) 639-4210

National Space Society
922 Pennsylvania Ave., SE
Washington, DC 20003
(202) 543-1900

Space Foundation
P. O. Box 58501
Houston, TX 77258
(713) 474-2258

Space Studies Institute
258 Rosedale Rd.
Princeton, NJ 08540
(609) 921-0377

Space Exhibits

The following air and space museums are a selected list and do not represent a complete guide. For space exhibits near your home, contact your local travel agent or chamber of commerce.

Alabama Space and Rocket Center
Tranquility Base
Huntsville, AL 35807
(800) 633-7280;
in Alabama, (800) 572-7234

California Museum of Science
and Industry
Aerospace Museum
700 State Dr., Exposition Park
Los Angeles, CA 90037
(213) 744-7400

Goddard Space Flight Center
Greenbelt, MD 20771
(301) 344-8101

Henry Crown Space Center
Chicago Museum of Science
and Industry
57th St. and Lake Shore Dr.
Chicago, IL 60637
(312) 684-1414

Johnson Space Center
Public Services Branch, AP4
Houston, TX 77058
(713) 483-4321

National Air and Space Museum
Smithsonian Institution
Washington, DC 20560
(202) 357-1552

Reuben H. Fleet Space Theater
and Science Center
Balboa Park, PO Box 33303
San Diego, CA 92103
(619) 238-1233

Spaceport USA
Kennedy Space Center, FL 32899
(305) 452-2121

BIBLIOGRAPHY

Caprara, Giovanni. *The Complete Encyclopedia of Space Satellites*. New York: Portland House, 1986.

Covault, Craig. "Soviet Cosmonauts on Mir Plan EVA to Repair Science Instrumentation," *Aviation Week and Space Technology*, June 27, 1988, 32.

Dorr, Les, Jr. "The Salvage of *Salyut 7*," *Space World*, May 1986, 8.

Eberhart, J. "Back to the Max: The Salvation Option," *Science News*, Aug. 6, 1988, 87.

McAleer, Neil. *The Omni Space Almanac*. New York: Ballantine Books, 1987.

NASA. *The Annual Report of the Goddard Space Flight Center*. Greenbelt, MD: NASA, 1988.

Scott, William B. "NASA Pressed to Attempt Second Solar Satellite Rescue," *Aviation Week and Space Technology*, Nov. 28, 1988, 36.

Waldrop, M. Mitchell. "A Bad Week for Soviet Space Flight," *Science*, Sept. 16, 1988, 1429.

Yenne, Bill. *Encyclopedia of U.S. Spacecraft*. New York: Exeter Books, 1985.

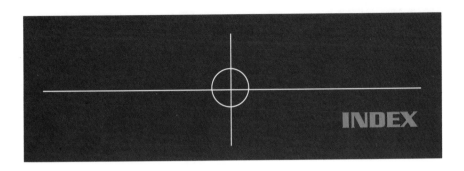

INDEX